TELLING EACH OTHER
IT IS POSSIBLE

Rosalind Brackenbury

TELLING
EACH OTHER
IT IS
POSSIBLE

TAXVS

ACKNOWLEDGEMENTS:

some of these poems have previously been
published in **Blind Serpent, Cencrastus, Chapman,
Other Poetry, Omens, Resurgence, Seeds &
Crystals, Spare Rib, Stand,** and **Writing Women.**

ISBN 1 85019 038 0

First published 1987 by
TAXVS PRESS,
Stamford Arts Centre,
27 St. Mary's Street,
Stamford,
Lincolnshire PE9 2BN.

The publisher gratefully acknowledges the financial
assistance of Lincolnshire & Humberside Arts

Typeset by Taxus Press
and printed by The Russell Press,
Bertrand Russell House, Nottingham NG7 4ET.

CONTENTS

TODAY

Today I saw the stones of this city
Were not grey but honeyed in the light;

Today there were daffodils in shop doorways
Tight bundles of sap and gold;

Today the wind blew clouds away like rags
And the sky was brilliant;

Today I thought of you
And your wide smile warmed me;

Today in the sun's flourish I wrote of you.

JOURNEY WITH FRIEND

Sleep is not yet as easy as we'd thought
On these two beds like fields, listening
To the time between the last drunk and the first
   dustbin,
Words spaced, tentative, our brief dreams
Opened easily by children's cries still
And the night movements of men.
Hands and mouths pluck at us,
We wake bewildered.

At my friend's, in the high room
Smelling of nappies, we slept
Like shoes in a box, my eyes at her feet,
Talked of ghosts as the bed creaked,
Heard her Mum and Dad rumble in the kitchen
Unfamiliar as snoring; wanting to pee
Or touch myself, scalded with bathwater
I dared not move, but boasted
Later, that I'd stayed awake all night.

And sat up later still, eighteen,
Straightbacked, writing our diaries, beehives
Like carapaces, hairpinned, dirty, eyes
Smarting with smoke, breathed in so's
Not to touch each other's thighs, though
The bed hammocked us at last like babies
And the bog flushed all night;
Enterovioform on the bed table and not enough
Cash for pain-au-chocolat, we smoked and wrote
The names of boys and bars and foreign songs,
Preserving everything, careful as widows.

Now, we take showers and taxis, gaze
In at Daniel Hechter rather than crème
Patissière, and find our faces strangely lined and
   gaunt
Against that healthy bloom of luxury;
Let moments pass, buy on impulse
In hundred franc notes, and wake to worry at two;
See skin sag, hands grow rough and veined
And mirrors welcome and then send us back.

Yet facing outward, streetward still
These years later in the known bar
I see our doubles in the glowing dark
Reflected; ironic, beautiful,
Turning without surprise this time
Towards the opening door.

HOKUSAI

The wave lifts, curls
Will break, scattering foam;

The petals will blow from these flowers,
Already the wind stirs

And here come the hurrying horsemen
Ducking their heads for speed,

Look — the moment is gone,
Look — where the leaves fly,

Sunset again at the end of the street
Scatters clouds in different directions

And there, you say, is the lake with the unruffled
    surface,
There is the eternal calm horizon line
And Mount Fuji, turning only
Through all the stages of incandescence
And back to ashen blue, burning
Yet never burned.

You lived with a mountain
There at the bottom of your street
Making it easier perhaps
Not to be temporarily blinded
By the storms of leaves, petals, tears?

DREAMS

Sometimes
Five floors up, behind those tall doors
Where the grey shutters open outwards
Floor's polished and music flies
Outward, you are at a party.
Only my pulse tells me you are here,
You see me, or do not see me,
Either way, I am pretending.

The mask hurts
Beneath it the quick running
Flush of passion: do you remember?

Last night she was showing us
Photographs in colour of my country,
Mud and wind, stamped by horses,
Locked by a savage sea
That makes you too a foreigner:

My land, your hand, her images
Of me, and I enclosed in them;
She shows, and we admire,
I, wary as a cat before a mirror
While she says only — look.

What are you doing, silent
As ever between two women? I cannot see,
Only feel the familiar exhaustion
Of avoiding your eye.
See, these pictures are yours, hers,
You have conquered me,
Decoded, simplified; there remains
Only the language of these hills.

FROM THE BLURRED MEMORY.   Aix 1975.

From the blurred memory
And the forgotten dream
From the inability to recognise
The reluctance to wonder
From the dull morning
And blindness in mid-afternoon
From too much looking
Too much remorse
From man at the centre of his world
Looking for what else to destroy:

Red squirrel leaping up at pinebark
Nightingale whistle at midday
Blackbird upon the cypress
All that is varied, myriad, complex and diverse
Save us.
From uniformity
From the extinction of species
From the aridity of an emptying world
From loneliness.
Striped caterpillar
Hornet, bumble bee
Large black and small red ant
Spider, centipede, lizard upon stone
Snake in the couch grass
Swallow above standing corn
Diving magpie
From our image in the empty glass
And from the silent stream
From ourselves somnambulating
Save us.

LOOKING FOR WORDS

looking for words plain enough to tell the truth
looking through water for the round brown stone
I find the weight here in my palm, itself alone

touch where the word may falter
earth marked with a passing tread
grass blown flat from many partings
the wild trees' circumference

touch of wind and the sky opens
step and the rabbits leap and bounce away
glance and the heavy partridge rise before you
there is your cold hand warming
this space, this time
my fields, your foreign land

rooted here as a scarecrow
alone now, arms spread, no way
to keep the wind out or close
what is laid open
flayed by the seasons
bone upon earth I let
the winter wheat grow up between my toes
and watch the wild hares run
lit in this sun between rain clouds

looking for words plain enough to tell the truth

CARD TRICK

Play, play cards — look!
I am the queen of magic.

Kneels in the dust now
Fingers flip as a croupier's
Deft as a trick: King
Queen, Jack, all — fly,
Fall, must lie at last
Flat, slick; ah, all come
Together, bedded, settled, wedded;
I am the queen of magic!

And her knees press
Hair flies and settles; rising
She is creased as an unfolded fawn
Swigs somebody's dregs
Takes bottles like a pirate
As the night blackens
Touches pale moth fingers
To cheeks, thighs;

Blazes eyes
Alert as trimmed lamps
Swung high above childhood:
Hi! Truth, dare; sure, fire;
See my desire
I am the queen of magic!

GREEN BOAT

all night there
and all early morning
rocking the grey wave
rocking and not sinking
breasting slap and hurt
again   again at bows
at battered sides   riding
this awkward strength of hidden tides
tugging the soaked rope taut
and letting slack again
riding   riding the wave

oh yes I found what I needed
all right if you should ask me
there at the tunnel mouth of bending trees
rain sluicing gutters to the sea
this morning's old green boat
and fatigue of that movement
to calm my steps back to you

FUNAMBULES.   Aix.

She wore a blue star on one cheek
Was lemur-eyed, pale beneath spangles
Leapt in a first long skirt;
And he, small clown, grinned
At the gilded goat, danced
In his way and rode at shoulder height;

Above us the fish-man swam
Silvered between layers of dark plane
His feet exploding in fireworks
Flame in his gullet; there for an hour
Pacing the laced void.

Distanced, you looked back at me
Russian-bearded in some grandfather's striped silk;
We balanced still above what might have been
Needing all that exactness of disguise.

FOR A WRITER'S CHILDREN

I see you go, in other directions
Down through the wet grass on Sundays
At a time — afternoon — when families
When couples, when children —
Through the garden gate and out, I see you go.

The house, as suddenly emptied, settles around me
And once again time opens fresh as a box of pencils
At once there is possibly
(You whom I love in your absences)
A way forward (as your outward footprints track my
    page);
Eased of you as after a long labour
Myself again, flat-bellied, taut, knit
To my own purposes, I sit behind glass
At a table with yellow chrysanthemums.

Silence comes that is not ringed and rippled
With your voices, but pooled for deep fishing.
You are not here to reproach me,
I breathe out as once, tiptoeing from your rooms
Nightly with fingers crossed I breathed,
Gambled for time and lost with a bad grace.

Older, you expect less but look angrier
As others, mothers, pack thermos flasks
Sandwich in outings, Sundays, when couples
When parents, when families —

Yet how will you know that I love you now
Unless seeking the word that will truly draw
Your mackintoshed backs departing
I can let you go?

MUSE

If I am to do without you
What space is made
What opening revealed?

Outside my house
A rink of hazard, ice
Knobbed and ridged with snow;
All morning the low sun
Slightly thaws.

I live at the edge of the sea
Where water would cut with cold;
Yet this is no excision
Rather a slipping away
On the outward, carrying tide.

What once is given
Can never be removed,
Nothing will stop the tidal suck.

But ice: and the need
That cracked my life across
Making the going hard.

I'll learn to walk
And look around at what is actual
Make conflagration of the past
Years and fingered memories and times
And times and secrets.

Fires upon ice. I'll rid
My imagery of yours
Empty my words of the burning glance
And live in my orderly days

Speak my own language
Open my door to strangers
Not wait to take your writing
Blurred with snow from
The postman's stiff mitten

I'll dream and wake untroubled
Cherish reality
Know all that fiery energy
My own, not granted, not given.
The sun, strengthening the morning
Making rivers in the street.

WHAT WAS ONCE FILLED

What was once filled
Is open to the air: today
The walls are down, today
Hunger begins to feel
Like receptivity. I throw
The windows up and let in
With the sun, blackbird song,
Another emptied season.

The gap your absence carves
Arches like a cathedral
May crack the bone
Is all space and light
Suddenly; there are those great holes
Smoothed out in bronze to astonish.

Yes, a woman is all space
Between the bones, the promontories
And around the heart;
Nothing clogs or lingers
There are only the insistent sculpted hollows,
The new dimensions.

My body takes strange positions
In an antique row of others
Schooled to the sharpness
Of what is unfamiliar,
Moves differently. I long for:
Form, resonance
All that we are not used to
All that stretches us
Pulling apart frailties
Letting in a strength that is like the sky.

THE MOON AND THE CLOCK FACE

full moon
and the clock on the kirk tower:
this cold, deep as sleep;
what lives, still at the centre
as the hands move, clocking the night?

I have emptied out
my cluttered heart
at the full moon
it spills upon the pavement
where we hacked and spread salt
at sunset;

the thawed spaces
blacken, spread,
there is a cracking
and a shiver of ice;
the curved black horse
on the pedestal trails icicles
from a raised perpetual hoof,
has frosted ears

in effigy, and I
sting hot with cold, where stones
go all the way down steep
to the pale waiting sea

the clock says: stop
and the moon says: forever,
there is only so much time, or:
there is eternity
in which all things may flow

on, says the white moon
and the bright clock says, no.

TO WOMEN PAINTERS OF INTERIORS

Crossing the polished floors of galleries
I come to your wide windows to look out
On gardens, fences, balconies,
Cap naps on faded wicker,
Washing lines, wheelbarrows,
Lace of blinds and rail and flower and leaf.

The curtains fold and curl
And light plays tricks with all
The fruit of your still life,
Hallows the chipped jug, Mary-blue,
And petals dropped like cream
On cloth that's soft and washed.

Thirsting for this
For things rubbed smooth with care
I follow you, the sunshine falling slant,
Into a woman's room, the shutters just ajar,
The sea and all my weariness locked out
With that black gust to rattle at the locks;

Nothing's undone or loosened here,
Cats doze, your work's on view,
Honesty pods scatter and the dream's
Of childhood, illness, meals on trays,
A fever stilled, and days slowed by my growing.

Are you my mother? Are you my own self?
You give me peace, not energy,
And stack your comforts round; I want
To finger things, sift through your button box,
Arrange your silks, fit scissors, thimbles,
Play among the spaces you have made.

Who is it, then, who stirs and paces in these rooms?
Whose voice is it that shouts to shatter glass?
Who's to account for that black raging sea out there
And mark the daylong passage of the sun?

SCULPTURE, EXHIBITED AT ORLY AIRPORT

in here is grounded
quiet and dark

beneath white lights
your fingers sliding
down the grainy flank
describe some birth

colder than flesh
the stones you shaped
your polished silences

in late night privacy
cast their true shadow

following you
my hand discovers
newness   surprised
by hidden clefts of stone

there are the cracks   openings
where life might spurt

also the solid mass
defying translation
itself alone

no word for that

watching I know myself touched
silenced
words will come later
landmarks of desire
charting the years

they stand where we leave them
our monuments
inscrutable standing stones
in deserts of white lights and passersby

LINDISFARNE

Come
In the soft grey afternoon
As far as the sea mark
Look, where the seals nose up;

Dusk
Is this simple gathering
Of sea and sky

The Farne light's
Suddenness what makes night
Come;

The turning point
Here, now,
The world deciding.

Upon the shore
Watching the slight frilled wave
Waiting for the whisper of it
The incoming tide,

We have come
As far as we may
And stand now backed
With this solidity
And know it, it comes,
It is in the still air
The turning.

Look, where those three dark birds flit past
Close trimmed upon the water face.

ORDER

order was made
but not strenuously
a clean polishing
of surfaces, the years scoured
made beautiful
no room for dust, stains,
the old shoe under the bed:

harmonies, rather
hour following hour
and the long dusk tranquil:
I would if I could
have made this, lived
and written it clearly
upon white sheets
upon days;
it was there
the first promise of all
before blood and dirt were let
before anxiety:

it was
a smoothness, apple-sure
sweet congruity
in which no stain was possible
no word too much;
a cleaned house
a ceremony attained:

the voice said
this is who you are
take it or deny it
what you inherit
this long cleanliness of days
this sky purity
hold it to your palm
fresh as ironed linen
pour it
fill the cold cup with what it is:
drink it, drink it down.

THE SEAL WOMEN

(from a traditional
Scottish story)

The cold sea it is that knows me,
The water my lover as no man can be.

Fifteen years I waited in your houses
Dry-eyed in your beds
Awaiting transformation;

I am almost changed, almost:
But winter evenings pace by the cold strand
Picking from wet sand what the sea has left.
The horizon closes its low gleam
As I go home.

On other beaches I see them,
The women whom the sea has reached;
In their kitchens, through their shutters,
Whispered to them at their winter firesides
Lured them singing from beds and embraces.

While we are in your arms, yes and
Holding children, setting the table,
It is there, there is no forgetting it;
How can I say this to you who have so loved me?

The day of my marriage I forswore the sea
Turned inland, drew blinds, lit lamps
Awaited instructions.
I thought it could be done, the salt rank passion
Purged and tidal pull annulled,
Water and its urgency be stilled at last,
Water that carried my breasts weightless
And spread my fingers, gave my body speed,
That entered me all ways, washed out my womb
And slapped my buttocks flat
Carried me as the wind splays bird flocks
Pulsing in the slip stream
Made me one of many, moved as one.

I am one of them, the seal women,
There are others,
Wives, mothers, daughters,
Pacing the shore of this island
For the incoming tide
Waiting till the gap of sea and rock is closed
Waiting till there are no more margins.

I hear them sometimes, the others,
They were wedded to the sea in their infancy
Girl children left too long on the uncovered sand,
The sea has stroked between their shoulder blades
And washed their dark heads smooth
Already; they are won
They are the free swimmers
Nights they struggle with the sea in their souls
It washes and floods their dreams
Woken by the moon they turn and tremble
The men they sleep with fling out hands
Across the bed, and dread to find them gone.

They have daughters
And their daughters plunge easily in
Into the small waves, their wet heads round
And eyes staring with pleasure;
One day their daughters
Or their daughters' daughters
Will not return.

And here are the emptied houses
The kitchens, bedrooms, food cupboards
Chairs upturned; here is a house ransacked
For the one thing needed.
Daughter, little daughter,
Tell me where it is
My skin, that was taken from me
In love; tell me where it is, my freedom.

TELLING EACH OTHER IT IS POSSIBLE

Telling each other it is possible
From firesides where we sip tea
Suddenly we are launched.

Suddenly it is a street wet with dawn
In the silence before doors opening.

Suddenly it is this blue, this clarity,
And we are beyond, somewhere else,
Looking down on other countries
Worlds, seas, rivers coasts
Where waves make only a faint white seam
And another country is only an edge.

Our life is become this
Seeking of destinations
Crossing of boundaries
Floating above coastlines;
You are the one, you said,
Giving my parachute a tug
So that the silk loosed
Carried me upon the air:
Dreaming at your kitchen fire one minute
And the next, beside me in the cold.
As we said good night, accomplices
Upon the step, some portion of the world
Fell easily to our inheritance.

Now, I change language, time, place,
Am drained, a chameleon, and sweat
With changing colour, with becoming;
I am at the edge
The dying light's a purple grain
And steps precisely tap on pavements
Going somewhere, at evening.
I shake, I sweat, I am dry-mouthed
With becoming.   I become.

I am all of you

I shake my dice at firesides
Where the paint dries and children sleep,
I climb to my lone tower room
Keeping the seas at bay.
— Yes, it's all very well at twenty
One can take the rough with the smooth
But at our age we expect quality
Or waste our time.

I am she who sits before a table
Fine brow slightly lined, and pours
Darjeeling from an ancient pot,
Gathers her hair at the nape
And opens a window inward, gazing
Past geraniums. into a closed courtyard.

Exactly.
I am she too who sits at a café table
Saying — yes, but how do you know
If you are any good?

Tonight as the dusk falls,
All of you. I am become you.
I cross your paths, in becoming
Perhaps myself.

Why here, now?
As the steps go down the street
And evening opens into heat
And I go out, daring:

Seas clouds coasts lands rivers islands
Cities. Lovers within cities.
Rooms where the window swings gently
Open to let in more light.
Chink of knives and plates, voices at evening.
Mealtimes families embraces voices
Doors opening closing
Lights from behind doors behind shutters

And then
One light and then
Voices again   laughter   indrawn breath   and then
Darkness   and then

Sleep

The polished and the rough surfaces
The smooth and easy   and the hard going.
Waking to another day
With that canvas to light
That stone to shape
That line to follow
That word to find
And that   and that   and that
And on   and on
That hand to take
That mouth to close
That   plate to fill   darkness to account for
Curtain to draw   circle to make   fire to tend
Hearth   home   habit   habit of loving
Loving
Loving of making
Making   making   making
Always   your lives
Something from nothing
Lump   dough   clay   experience
Stuck in the throat
Tears   fears   desires
To seize   use
You who are grasping
Grasping   not flinching
Brands   burning irons
In case it is necessary
In case it might be required

And then   tossing lightly all this
Aside   run down a street in sunshine after a child
Singing three notes of a song

FORESTS AND CLEARINGS

I think often now of forests and clearings –
Trees new-felled with a downward stroke
Echoes in the wood, and a white spur left, sap
    bleeding,
The barred circles to show how time passed
Till now.

There are the flattened grasses
In a place ringed by trees; space carved
Where none was, and the silence of waiting,
Of what comes. Far sounds excluded,
A world close-circled, charmed,
Into which no beasts pass.

There was the small fire you built
Taking dried twigs first, the smallest,
Your careful nurturing of flame;
This I had not imagined
Flame turning all solid things to mirage
A hand stretched skyward making the tall trees
    bend.

There is the exactness of it
This small space,
For a brief nomads' encampment, pitched
Against all probability, for an hour or two
The centre of the known world
In which all things are possible.
Afterwards, trees spring back and new shoots grow,
The grass grows faster, washed by an hour's rain
And ash and earth are quickly mingled back;

The spot's not marked, the forest will reclaim it;
I think easily now of forests and clearings.

Within these four walls, door
Locked for a while and window full of swallows
And plane trails on sky; here was
A meeting, parting, unrecorded
Cries and laughter lost to the still air.

I think — we might gnaw bones, draw in the ash
With sticks, squat close and search each other's
Skin and eyes, wondering what is human,
Finding answers in a rawness of experience
Never before —
Knowing only what is new, like our first ancestors,
Hand's grasp a newness
Flame struck surprising as dawn
And each sun-up relief and revelation —

Bone to bone socketed, eyeball close
The rivers stream and dry
The hand knows exactly, finally
Fits as the first toolmaker's, flesh to stone
And transforms easily loose matter into
What is sculpted, perfectible,
A festival of form; freed, struck into orbit
Springs away, invisibly circling the earth forever.

I think — in such clearings, life flared and died
Always, and what remained, cut stones,
Bared bones, the painted beasts' flourish
On the walls; signs, inheritances;
Where words failed and the winter dark was long
From the first fearful touch to the
Brave new trackways of pleasure
Knowledge forged from fresh pacts and hand
And brain, just so, always.

And the birds dived overhead, calling,
And the next time and the next remained unknown.

BAMBOIS.   For Claudie, 1981.

1.   In your house where flowers
Bunch from the beams and bracken dries
And the green plant transforms
Hourly, daily, and all is
Becoming; where the dogs smile
On the threshold
And so many pairs of shoes
Hint at arrivals;
I come in barefoot now
Thankfully
And partake in infusions
Transformations
Amnesties.

2.   Here is the clearing
There between the close trunks leaning
Here on the soft grass
There where the sun darts briefly
Shall it be?
I await something — man
Or animal, some hint of music,
Whatever might step fully grown
From behind that tree;
But there is lit grass only
Berries brilliantly garlanding the rowan
And the silence
Cracks like a full nut
Scattering the moment.

3.   Tiptoeing through fern
Beneath tall trunks of pine
They come, russet young females
Like girls entering a room;
We look at each other
For a full minute,
I stand still as the trees
And they move on
Threading a bright strand
On the trees' loom
Weaving the forest alive.

4.   Waking this early
To a world bowl rimmed
With blue mountains
Trickle of cold water
And the chill bell chime
I stand ankle deep in wet grass
Relishing the first burning sip
Of morning.

FOR MY DAUGHTER:
ECLIPSE OF THE MOON

When the slow stain covered the moon
Nearly, I thought of blood;
It was ice-bright that night
And air too sharp to breathe.
We stood with feet numb in snow
Holding each other like savages
Watching the stars in their accustomed places
And this freak, this marvel.

All evening at the uncurtained window
Where cold stuck to the pane
She aimed her telescope to the moon
Seeking its imperfections; with indrawn breath
Searched the night sky for it
Peach-bloom, rose-glow, bloody fruit,
Looking for knowledge exact enough to satisfy.
It is just a shadow, she said,
While I thought of blood
And the relief change brings.

Out in the transformed garden
Flicker upon white, our indoor fire
Bloomed strangely cold and eternal
As imitations do. Hours later
Towards midnight, the moon swung clear
In a changed sky; and we drew curtains,
Turned inward to warmth again,
Wearied of miracles. Elated with facts
And the moon's power, she slept.

FOR MY GOD-DAUGHTER,
WHO BROKE MY BRACELET

Night begins on the marsh path
Thickening from dusk.
You trot a straight way through
Telling of butterflies while owls call
Talking of favourite clothes and foods, till 'Cow!'
You cry, and run at the ghost face and horns
Till the gate gives a limit, hurtle
From fear to safety, you at the centre
Of your great world again, feeling its boundaries.

Getting to know you
I am almost glad you broke it so easily
Firm fingering that heavy alien thing,
My bloodied ivory, dead weight hinged
Far too flimsily with silver.
(Animal, vegetable, mineral?
Slave or free?) I would not
Have you seek beauty in such imbalances
But see life demand bone and jewel
Weighed equally.

Take and break, Elaine, let fall with equanimity
All that my come within your roaming hand
With such ambivalence.

THE WELL

The crowbar prises bricks apart,
Red dust spatters, cracks
The pattern as the great slab
Sealed with weeds comes up;
We lever shadow from the inside earth,
Peer down to distant water,
Unknown quantities, gallons;
A pebble sounds echoes,
A single word.

Cold secret depths.
We hang a bucket, skim and taste,
A rite. Thirst is endless
And the pools run dry.
You say, sweet water, it is clear,
Uncoloured, you can see right through.
The house has found its soul
And we shall pump it, slaking
The dried earth, greening the willow.

We straighten up to stare
In sudden twilight; here
Was no divining stick
But quick, old memory.
Before the dark falls
You cover it with a slate slab
Marked for cheesemaking with its clear mandala.

FOR SAM RIDING

Jockey-high you nod
Palm lines greased with horse flesh
Wind at your ribs knocking
World bowl sky filled.

Little earth worm you crawled
So long beneath tables, at doorstops,
Tracked across airless plains of carpet;
Now your line forms, hill rises.

Horses will carry you on like water
Between the thighs, yet are solid,
Your real other; up here
Only the clouds top you;

Child astride the muscled universe
Between hoofbeat and pulse
Feel the real world enter.

AT ENTREMONT

The city falls,
The great press cracks across
A way of living
Stone split into two worlds;
Between, this.

Oil runs still from the crushed fruit,
There is no end to movement.

He was here and is not,
No more nor less
Than they of the fallen city.
Our feet ignorantly pace
Soft grass above streets, rooms
Where the hearth stone stands

Still, the thumbed pot and the trodden sill;
time turf-bedded, inaccessible.

Birdsong and the clear morning
Inform us: he to she
to he to me
the link is, will be,
to see and feel now
All that is needed.

EDINBURGH FEBRUARY

Yesterday's flakes of flying snow
And seagulls, wings against the wind
As whiteness settled on the city's grey:

Out there in the cold I was
Taking the cold head on and walking fast,
Pitted against what came, and set that way;

Then night-time came your voice
Softer than falling snow in darkness
Speaking peace, telling me let what comes
Flurry and settle gently, let it be.

Striving and high they circled in the air
Those wild birds driven from the icy sea
Silenced at last by softness.

Yesterday's flakes of flying snow
And seagulls, wings against the wind:
Today's bright silences.

RAPHAEL

He waits, eyes only just above table height;
His brother spikes a forkful.
You watch, father at the table head;
The knife quivers in the running meat
Garlic-slivered; wine warms.

'Bouffes ta viande, Raphael
Ou t'auras mon pied dans le cul.'

Yesterday on the synagogue steps
The armed flic stamped in the cold
Shifting the white-sheathed pistol at his hip

The queues were for art, not religion,
Or so it initially seemed.

You watch his pained swallowing,
Would have him win at chess,
Outsmart you with his queen.

'Bouffes ta viande, Raphael, vite!
Pour être un homme.'

ON A TRAIN, READING MARINA
TSVETAYEVA'S LETTERS TO
BORIS PASTERNAK

Journeys, journeys are like —

Leaving by the back way on a train like a tram
I sit upright facing the front
Talking to you again, unwinding
My long monotone that coils and coils
And unwinds, telling you: look, I say,
There is the cathedral at Ely
Surprising from here, coronet beneath cloud,
There is a heron poised by the hedge
And harvesters prowl nibbling through fields,
Look, England at harvest, field and dyke
Of open fen, and the sky guileless,
Blue September, blond, cropped, windy;
What else matters?

Your language runs in me and shouts me down,
My own is full of gaps and fragments; I am
Hardly able to speak aloud, yet record,
Expert at simultaneous translation
Giving everything away, even
The secret yeast that makes poetry,
Field and house and station separate, gone.
And I would make you not of then but now,
Not there but here — look, this is the present,
It passes fast enough.
What is it that I would tell you of myself
Through this passing landscape, its urgency?

Reading her letters to him, I think —
We are all, all driven, and by this pain.
Look, she was saying, and listen, listen to me;
She was one of many, Marina Tsvetayeva,
Women, I mean, not poets, laid bare and sad
In her letters, yet in her poems proud.
Boris, Boris —   Reading her, I pass through
This landscape, telling you.

The day is hot.   We change at March.
Station a daze of autumn sunlight.
People are separate from each other
And in the carriage an old man who settles
Takes off his shoes.

Marina Tsvetayeva, I say, we do not have to,
Do not have to share it all
Or hold nothing back, we do not have to
Speak hopelessly in another language
Begging for what we already have;
We do not have to explain everything . . . .

He gives me a crazed pottery box,
This old man, wrapped in fine tissue.
I lift the lid. It is empty. Empty
But beautiful. I give it back
And he smiles, closing his eyes,
Gets out at the next stop.
There is the airless empty heat of afternoon.
I think — we are incomplete creatures
All of us, and when we lose our voice, helpless
Except to move slowly on across the unfamiliar.

HOLY LOCH, JANUARY

staring up
into such depth and grey
of unfamiliar sky
I think of sunbathing

translate the earth's iron
touch at my spine

imagine, lying naked on hot sand?

no longer white on blue
the seagulls drop and rise
as if we were crumbs or fish

there is a terrible stillness
of white mountains today
a terrible cry of birds

anything could be
down in the deep sea loch
anything

snow gathers in the fleet cloud
deep cold; all the layers
fur leather mackintosh wool skin
could be peeled away

we lie flat
simulating death by cold fire
January on the coast of Scotland

next time I lie like this
belly up at the sea's edge
letting the sky in
can it be for thawing
not freezing
not this?

TURNER IN EDINBURGH, JANUARY

There at the heart
the molten gold
transformed, transforming;

here in the coal glow
furnaces stoked
against black rain;

darkness reddens each evening
into high festival,
pocks the cliff faces with lit cells;
there is the tug of tide and cloud
at what is bound;

early, the sky fills
these same windows with fire,
cools again into day.

There is what is ashen
and what is white with heat
and in between, the choosing;

where the sweep of heaven
matches all the rush of earth
there are no distinctions
only leaps, only bridges

and we wait
where the horizon was;
till then, the turmoil
breeds these pure cities, these dreams.

I wake at five
in my nest of towers
my hive of light;
fire is not yet behind the shutters
yet comes, is coming
as rain blows in from the sea,
here the palaces huddle in the wet
and only at dawn and windy sunset
start to rise and stream.

How was it then, to walk so lightly
always between soaring stones
knowing this lifted space in his own skull
to find all matter molten
without effort of alchemy
fleshed only with what was essential
life a lifting of hands
stone a dance of light?

Now in the stone city
easier between precipices
sky breaks the streets open again and again

BLAEBERRIES

Eating from our palms squashed blaeberries
lips stained, feet soaked
among the glossy leaves
we wandered further in
babes-in-the-wood style;
you said, this is how
people get lured into forests
you go just a little further
and a witch appears.

The old Scots pine before us twists and points
there was a gate
wasn't there?
but I don't remember this part
look — where a single horse
thudded uphill an hour ago
cast hoofprints deep in peat;

yet there is still the cold and far down burn,
and here a Japanese garden
squats, smooth rocks, a bright green fir
knee-high and Christmas spruce with cones
for candles; enough landmarks, surely?

you are looking at forests
with a new eye, a man with a map
trail-reading;
I am looking for old clues, but otherwise.

I am glad we stuck with it
you say as the sun comes out
and I roll my mackintosh
though sometimes I did wonder
what was the point;

you lick up the blue fruit like a Norseman
forgetting to smile
like this you are enough of a stranger
enough of a friend;
you have the map
and I the compasses
and, north, north, we say
pushing through undergrowth
surprised to find each time
we're facing south again:

today the hills are slate-black
below a slate-blue sky.
all the words I use are old
you know them
my intonations, my repertories;
how shall I surprise you?

yet we try
on the borders of forests
walking towards the edge
where Scotland ends in sea
to speak with the clear ring of axes
struck in wood
to make clearings.

Are you sure they are blaeberries
you ask suddenly, as I might
well have asked you, are you sure
we are going north?

Sure, I said,
in among the sharp and polished leaves.